100 EXCUSES for not doing THINGS

May Betom Horrow

Gadama

Preface

This book is dedicated to 4 people called EVERYONE, SOMEONE, EACH ONE and NONE.

There was a very important and difficult job to do and EVERYONE was sure that SOMEONE would do it.

EVERYONE could have done it, but NOBODY did.

Until EVERYONE blamed SOMEONE because NO ONE did what EVERYONE should have done.

So, the important thing is not that you are SOMEONE or NOBODY, but to have a good EXCUSE.

Index

Appendix	98
Capitolo 3 – 100 scuse per evitare di fare cose	72
Chapter 2 - 100 Excuses to Avoid Invitations	29
Chapter 1 - 100 excuses to be late	9
Index	5
Joke	96
New excuses	94
Notes on the author	100
Preface	3

100 and more, or less,
excuses for not doing
something or for someone
else to do it other than me or
someone who might ask me
again if I make myself available,
because I haven't found a new
excuse.

I would like to dedicate this book to
someone I know, but I don't want to

Chapter 1 - 100 excuses to be late

"... Excuses are like assholes, everyone has one ..."

Forget it, you wouldn't understand

I am arriving by train

Sorry I'm late, but as I left the house I remembered that it had been a long time since I had cleaned the lock on the door, and so I preferred to do it before forgetting again

I'm sorry, but since I learned to read hands, I spend a lot of time in the bathroom and I haven't noticed that I'm late

Sunday morning? I really can't, I have to replace the priest at mass

I don't think I'll make it in time, I have to help grandmother sort out the phone book again because the dog has mixed up all the sheets

I don't think I can come, I have the semi-finals of the toilet paper throwing championship, and I don't know how long they will last

No, I really can't, I have to bathe the cat tomorrow

I'm sorry but I can't come tonight, I just dropped my sister's puzzle and I need to fix it before I get back

Today is the anniversary of when my cousin opened his plastic cup factory and he would be offended if I didn't go to the party

The dog dropped the vase with my collection of marbles, now I have to collect them all

It wasn't expected, but I started playing Monopoly on the phone with my uncle who lives in Japan and until the game is over I can't go out.

You said 5 ... I'm sorry, I understood eleven ...

I saw BATMAN on the ring road and I took the wrong exit

I was up all night to find a good excuse for being late if I was late. Eventually, I fell asleep at 4 and woke up at 12 ... and I was late

No. Don't ask me anything. You would never believe it.

Didn't you tell me there was a curfew …?

But did you say via Verdi 2? Not 425 ??

I found a bird's nest and I need to feed it

Well, it seemed like a funny thing to arrive two days after the ceremony …

I stopped talking to Tom Cruise for two and a half hours and he didn't want to let me go

It is precisely because the work requires extreme punctuality that I wanted to blow you away by coming to the end of the interviews

I thought I arrived, but I haven't even left

A UFO landed on the ring road, half an hour to move it!

You said under the house in twenty minutes, but you didn't specify whose house

I was studying a possible solution for time travel and I wanted to prove that I had succeeded by starting late

Ah, the system was sexagesimal. You didn't specify it

CLOSE CLOSE! They have been chasing me for at least 2 hours!

I love moments of embarrassment, like this

I've been knocking on your neighbor's door for 2

hours, he also called the carabinieri

Do you remember Lugozzi? the one from 3rd high school, the one with the uncle with the bar? Well, you'll never believe it but I met him on my way here ... he stole my watch

Just an hour ago he called my mother from Japan to tell me that I am the reincarnation of Winston Churchill

Excuse me but just two hours ago you called me Winston Churchill to tell me you are my mother. I didn't believe it either, in fact, but we had a fight. During this time he intrudes too much into my private life and I had to remind him that I am no longer a child

Every latecomer has an excuse. I don't have it, so I'm not a laggard. Am I calling Aristotle?

Free not to believe me, but I died 2 hours ago

Sorry I couldn't go out because I was sleeping

Sorry I couldn't go out because I took my grandmother for a visit

Sorry but I was staying with relatives

I left work late

I was walking in the park with my grandmother

I was at the vet, I took my dog, which I adopted shortly before

I was in the bank doing a robbery and they detained me

Someone stole all my shoelaces

I was in the bank getting robbed

Sorry but I was picking up my cousin from school

I was cleaning my wife's car

I was at my girlfriend's house, even though she doesn't know she is

It's raining and I have to go slow in case it starts snowing

It's too hot and I have to go slow in case a storm comes

I punctured all 4 tires

I can't find parking and I stopped at the bar

I got lost in the bar

A patrol stopped me near the bar

There were demonstrators (no mask, no triv, no fat, no excuse ...)

I stopped for gas and it was closed

I missed the bus and I was also without a ticket

There was an accident between a lost bus and my car

I realized it was later

But hadn't we moved it to later?

Oh man, I thought the appointment was yesterday and I was

already late, so I took my time

You looked like you so I left

Sorry I'm late, I had the clock backwards

I was studying the phone book, tomorrow I have the exam

I didn't arrive late, I arrived too early and stopped at the bar

Sorry I'm late I was waiting for the yogurt to expire at midnight

Sorry for the delay but I was insulted by a bunch of grapes and I stepped on it

I found a needle and wasted a lot of time looking for the haystack

I would like to but I had a fight with Gino Paoli and 2 others

I was dubbing a silent movie

Until yesterday I had not been drinking 100 days ... they were

Look I called you

I was carrying the ancient vase to safety, I don't tell you what an effort

I was applying nail polish to my left hand

I had to walk, my dog took the car

Sorry but I have a very polite alarm clock and he

doesn't want to disturb me while I sleep

I asked for directions because I didn't remember the address and that guy sent me to the other side of town

Alexa didn't want to let me go

Look it's not my fault but I really don't know why but tonight I felt like going for a run, so I ran to the end of the road, and once there I thought I'd run to the end of town, then once there I thought about running through Greenbow County. Then I said to myself, since I got this far I might as well run through the beautiful state of Alabama and so I ran through all of Alabama; I ran to the ocean and, once there I said to myself, since I got this far I might as well turn around and keep running. Then when I got to another ocean, I said to myself, since I got this far, I might as well turn around again and keep running

Chapter 2 - 100 Excuses to Avoid Invitations

"... If God exists, I hope he has a valid excuse ..."

I just can't, my parents are out, I don't know when they're back and I have to look after my 25 year old brother

I don't want to go out... for example, I didn't even go out last week!

I can't go out because I already went out last night and my mom doesn't want to!

Let's do it next time because I left yesterday morning and came back this morning with the seven forty-seven train

*that arrives at eight forty-
one and so I'm tired*

*I just can't, my house has
flooded and I have to stay
here with the leaks until
the water runs out*

*I can't, I'm busy, I have to
go to the gym, see I also
have a card*

*Wait, I'll think about it, I'll
tell you in a while*

*I cannot go out because I
have workers who work in
the kitchen*

I'm not old enough to go out alone with you!

I already had another engagement, I tried to cancel it because obviously I prefer to go out with you, but I couldn't

But are you crazy, have you seen what the wind is?

I can't, I'm writing a list of excuses not to go out

We would ruin our friendship by getting to know each other better

I can't, my uncle ran away again and we're looking for him

I can't, I have to study for a very important blood test

I can't, a man on TV advised me not to change the channel for any reason

Look Saturday I have to go to the mountains, when I come back I will be very tired, in case I am not I have to decide where to go next time

It's a time I've been distracted by things bigger than me

I have to make decisions that I don't know how to make, so my perception of things seems so confused to me that I don't remember now you asked me

The last thing I would like to do is fool someone, whom I care a lot, just for fun

I don't deserve you so I'm doing it for you

I would love to but there are discounts at Mc Donald's and I can't miss them

It's not you that's not good for me, it's me that's not good for you

I love you too much to go out with you

But didn't you realize we are too different and too alike at the same time?

You have no idea how much I'd like to go out with you, but I just can't

I know you too well, I know what you need ... and I can assure you it's not me

I am forced to decline your invitation due to an unstoppable commitment that I am about to make right now

Sorry I didn't call you but the cat stole my phone

I can't wait to go out with you I tell you so many things! For example, do you know I have a new boyfriend?

Look, now I really don't have time ...

I can't have herpes and I feel very infectious

There is too much cultural difference between us

Sometimes I like being alone and now it's just one of those moments

I never go out when I am invited, I prefer to be the one to invite

But don't you feel like you're running too fast?

But what if you've only known me for 12 years?

My psychologist says I don't have to go out just because I've been invited

I wish I could but I have to make cheese

We are the usual, every time to go out is always the same story, so I don't go out

I can't, they hit my favorite socks yesterday

Better not, then I'm afraid you get too attached to me

I made a foil

I just can't go out tonight... you know I can't use deodorant because I just shaved my armpits

I can't, I found a leak in the bathroom and I'm plugging it with my finger

I'd love to go out with you, but I never go out in the first 23 hours of the day

I would love to go out with you, but right now there is my favorite commercial on TV

I was just about to call you back to decide what time to meet, but then I found out I didn't have your number

Look if I don't have to work, I'm definitely coming

I can't have to fold the sheets

I can't go out. I have to wax

Sorry but I can't go out because I have run out of car in reserve and I don't have money for gas

I'm sorry but I can't even tonight. I filled up with petrol, but my car is diesel, now the engine no longer starts

I'm sorry but we just can't see each other. During the day I work and at night I can't go out because my car only runs on solar power

The cat vomited me all over my shoes

I can't go out because I got Ebola

No, thank you but I stopped

Thanks, as if I accepted

Sorry, I just can't ... I'm running out of yogurt

After 9/11 I changed

It's not that I don't want to go out with you, it's just a logistical question too complicated to solve in the short time you have made available to me

I'm not gay

I am a lesbian

I don't want to get off to a bad start with the new year

Sorry, I'm already sleeping. This is an automatic reply

I am waiting for the Amazon courier

I can't today Mattarella called me to do the government

I can't have promised me a steady job

I can't tonight, I'm measuring when the water runs out at the bottom of the toilet

I'm sorry but I can't, I have to check that the clock always strikes the right time

My hair is dirty and if I wash it too often it will wear out

I can't tonight, I have to verify that they don't lie to

the Regina roll advertising,
I'm measuring them

I can't tonight, the flowers
you sent me are so
beautiful that I don't feel
like leaving them alone

I can't tonight, I have to
file my cat's nails

I can't tonight, I have to
queue the cat

I'm not there tonight, the
spider I had in the
basement is dead and I
feel too down

I can't tonight, I have to monitor my dog's hair growth

I can't tonight, I celebrate the centenary of the curfew and I don't go out if it gets dark

I can't tonight, I have to study for blood tests

I can't tonight, I have to monitor that the lunar cycle does not make mistakes

I can't go out with you, my religion which I just joined prevents me

You are too much for me and I don't deserve you

I really can't tonight, I feel winter is coming

I can't tonight, the letter for admission to Hogwarts is coming

I can't tonight, there is the 90th edition of the Hunger Games and this time I wanted to offer myself as a tribute

I can't tonight, I've alreadeaten

I can't today, Jehovah gets married and asked me to be his witness

I can't tonight, there is the thirty-fifth rerun of the fiftieth episode of Ciao Darwin

My mother doesn't want to tie my shoes and I fell

I live alone and I'm fine with it

I have an appointment with my extraterrestrial friend who passes me to pick up after 11pm

It would be great to go out with you, but my dog ate the keys and I don't know how to close the house

I wish but I didn't sleep a wink this morning at work

I would love to, but I dropped a jar of glue on me while I was in bed, now I'm stuck here waiting for the firemen

I would love to go out with you, but my foot has fallen asleep and I can't make any noise

NASA called me on a mission to save the world from an asteroid and I'm about to leave, ah don't tell anyone

A black cat crossed my street and I would risk my life leaving the house

The thieves have entered the house and they are still here having an aperitif

I don't have the right clothing to go out with you

Forget it, I'm in a bad mood and you could only make me worse

Sorry but I don't feel comfortable

Sorry but the match is there

Sorry but I feel terrible

Sorry but it's too late now

Sorry but it's too early now

I cannot leave the dog alone and I cannot take him out because I may meet someone allergic

I don't feel like going out because it's too cold this August

I don't feel like going out there is too much wind

I can't come there because it's too far away and I'm afraid of distances

I can't come this far because it's too far to even imagine it

I can't go out because I have a fever

I can't go out because I have a cold and I don't want to attack you

I can't go out because I have back pain

I can't go out because I'm nauseous from back pain

I can't go out because I have a cough from back pain nausea

I can't go out because my c ...

I can't go out because I have diarrhea

I can't go out because I have a toothache

I can't go out because I have a stomach ache

I can't go out because I threw up

I can't go out because I have a headache

I can't go out because my eye is bad

I can't go out because my bones are bad

I can't go out because my pea itches

I can't go out because it itches ...

I can't go out because I'm on my period and I wouldn't want you to use it as a commonplace for my character

I don't want to go out because I'm very nervous

I don't want to go out because today I'm boring and I don't want to meet other boring people

I can't go out because I'm apathetic today

I can't go out because my nail hurts

I can't go out because I have to go for gas

Sorry but I was going down the stairs I fell and found myself in China

I would love to come but I had to blow my grandmother's soup

I have tennis elbow and I should give it back today

I can't go out, I have my bike in reserve

I can't come to work I have the guinea fowl in the oven I'm waiting for the archaeologists

I can't come to work today, I woke up dead

I can't come, I'm at my funeral

I can't have to count my hair

I can't, they're calling me from the moon

I can't go on like this, I put it in reverse

I can't have to check if the sea is wet

Sorry for the delay I put the shoes backwards and I split in half

I can't come tonight I'm at Luca's house, Luca who?
....

I can't tonight, God invited me to dinner

I can't have to make a deposit to the sperm bank

I can't go out because my nails hurt

I would like to go out but people look at me

I can't come because they have to bury me and I'm already late

I can't, Mom doesn't want to

I can't get out, I'm broken and I'm done with the attack

I can't come today my dog graduates

I can't! I have to play cristal ball with Roberto Ball

I can't have found the words and I'm taking them to Ligabue

I wanted to write you, but I can't write and you can't read

I can't have to study for blood tests

The car did not start because there were rabbits in the cylinders

I can't come, I have to fill the camel with water

I have to go to Germany
to learn French

I can't come today maybe
they let Toto Cotugno sing

I can't, I'm very busy, I
have to count the squares
of a lined notebook

I can't go out with you
because I'm waiting for a
sitting bull to get up

I would like to go out with
you but you are not my
ideal type of CUD

Ah, did I tell you yes? Sorry you know ... the T9

Sorry but the gravitational field of my house is too strong to escape him

There is a time and place for everything ... and it is not the time

I'm under house arrest

I have the Winnie the Pooh concert tonight, I already have the tickets

Okay, but call me tomorrow

My computer got a nasty virus and I would like to stay home and treat it

I've decided I don't go out until I can kiss my elbow

Valentine's day? But you know I'm not a Catholic

I have to go wake the bears from hibernation

Unfortunately my mom no longer wants to tie my shoes

Look, it's not raining and it bothers me to leave the umbrella at home alone

I can't go out, are you crazy? salt spilled on the mirror broken by my black cat!

I'm sorry but my car tires are too inflated

Forget it, but tonight the wind is against

Don't wait for me, my health shirt has caught the flu

How do I get out? By now I have made myself a position on the sofa

I can't go out because I have to wake up early in the morning, I have to check that the sun rises

It is my plumber's name day

I can't go out, my legs are on strike and they crossed their arms!

I just lost 6 lives in Risiko, how do I get out?

I have the spare tire on the ground

Tonight I already have a commitment, I would like to listen to all the music on hold from the Vodafone call center

Are you crazy? Tomorrow is Tuesday and the day after tomorrow is Wednesday!

I can't, I'm too short

Look at Moscow it's snowing and I'd like to

avoid being out when it
gets here too

I'm sorry but I have to stay
in bed all day in the
morning

I have to reflect in the
mirror

I came up with a scary idea
for tonight, but I got it
right

I have the car is off now
and I would hate to turn it
on

I can't have said on facebook that there is covid

I forgot 1 euro in the shopping cart and I have to go back to find it

Tonight I would like to go to bed with a fever and I would not want it to go away when I come back

I'm not coming because I'm not handsome

I must become a nun

I drank too much vov

I must go buy the tuna to
cut it with a breadstick

Sorry but I have to check
if the sky is getting bluer

I wish I could, but I have
to go to the doctor to ask
who is the last

I must set the table for a
dinner for 13, but this
time is the last eh

Chapter 3 - 100 excuses for not doing things

"... Love is a great excuse, especially if it is mutual ..."

I need to check the expiration dates of everything I have in the fridge

My cat suffers from vertigo and I must check him when he gets on the furniture

I was swimming too fast and hit my head on the edge of the pool

My hamster died

I got hurt doing great sex ... alone

I am hallucinating and I see people asking me to do things

I'm stuck in the house because the door broke

My new girlfriend bit me in a very delicate spot

I burned my hand on the toaster

The dog ate my shoes, all of them

I would like to but my batteries are dead

My fish is sick, he has a cough

I swallowed the white spirit

My big toe got stuck in the tub faucet

I'm in the ER with a clothespin on my tongue

Mom doesn't want to

I drank too much, fell asleep and now I'm on the floor of someone's house, I don't know where I am

My pants broke on my way to work, now I'm trying to change his mind

I am using a new contact lens solution and my eyes are watering with emotion

My nose is stuffy and I can't get out

I made a mess of hair dye

I have a sore finger and I won't tell you the rest

For privacy, I can't tell you

I have a medical certificate

Give me a reason why I make money out of it

I have to listen to the mass on the radio

Now I can't, I have to pick up the pencil behind the desk and I can't find it anymore

I have to go home, I seem to hear my alarm ring

My car was stolen

My car was scratched while it was stolen from me

I crashed my car into yours

I'm on my way to the post office and plan to stay there until tomorrow

My alarm did not go off and I'm revising it

I'm going to wash my teeth

I can't, I'm looking for a hat because I no longer have a hair

I have a dentist appointment and he wants me to brush my teeth

The light's out, but he doesn't want to go down

I asked Scarlett Johansson to meet on Tweeter and have been waiting for an answer for 6 months

I'm directing a movie

I have an audition for the new 007

My eyes are burning

It burns my c ...

I have to go out with a girl
who will definitely give it
to me

I don't know what time it is
anymore

I have to go pay the bills

I have to go play soccer

I've never done it and now
I don't have time to see
how it's done

I didn't know it was urgent

It is not my responsibility

Nobody gave me the OK

I am waiting for the OK

I didn't know it was important.

I have so much of that stuff to do that I just can't do this too.

My phone dropped from the balcony

Haven't I already sent it to you?

Today I can't, I have to look for the lost souls with Piero Pelù

My mail doesn't work

The pc does not turn on anymore

The phone here does not have signal

I left the cat on the pressure cooker

Self-driving my car doesn't want to take me to work

My sauce burns

My boss is calling me

The Wi-Fi went out

I'm writing a book of excuses

I can't do it since it's raining and I'm afraid of getting sick

I'm waiting for the cleaver from heaven

I can't leave the dog alone

I can't. I'm watching a great movie on the radio

My parents don't want to!

I have to go kill some lactic ferments

I have to keep an eye on the goldfish, I think one of them intends to commit suicide by jumping out of the bowl

I don't feel like going out because I'm afraid that someone will look at me badly

I found a newborn in front of the front door, now I have to raise him and make him a responsible adult like me

I have a strong intestinal virus, I'm ashamed without my bathroom

I can't go out, I have to get up early in 5 days

My glasses are broken and I can't find the spare ones because I can't see them

I have to calculate the centripetal acceleration of

the balls when they spin
me

I have to go to my great-
uncle's condominium
meeting

I was locked in the
elevator

I'm still in the casino, still
winning

I'm making the stew and I
have to follow it

I woke up in a good mood
and wouldn't want to spoil
it

I'm flying on a plane that I got on by mistake

I find myself in a house that is not mine

I can't see without glasses

I opened my eyes and now I can't close them anymore

I can't have to find out where the sun goes to sleep

I'm afraid the earth will explode

Can we do it another time? There is the game soon

I can't now, I'm working

I can't, my shoulder hurts

I took the wrong door, it was a window

Now I have to go to the bathroom

I would like to pass but you are too bulky

And how do I do this? The power went out

My cousin's brother-in-law has lost the canary and I have to help him find it

I can't now, I'm listening to the brake discs

I can't come to work I have the guinea fowl in the oven I'm waiting for the archaeologists

Sorry I have to go away, I thought it was a fart

I can't crown my cavalier king today

I don't feel tastes and smells

I can't, I'm in bed with measles and I don't want to leave him alone

My car radiator brake broke

But don't worry, there is so much time

I broke the chair on a friend's back and I need to fix it

Sorry but I can't do it, I'm translating my book into all the languages of the world

I'll do it later, I promise

Sorry you don't feel ..
there must be a ... blem with the ... inea

The man from the mountain said NO! You understand it?

I have the pc in service

Sorry there's my favorite Thai soap opera on TV

Excuse me, they're calling me

I can't, today I have to stock up for the end of the world

My mayonnaise went crazy and I have to cure it before it gets hurt

They say the acceleration of gravity is 9.81m / s2 I have to jump from a building to see if it's true

New excuses
Practice finding new excuses and jot them down here

Joke

At the university, a professor was finishing giving her students the latest information on the final exam they would take the next day. She finished by saying that there would be no excuse for not showing up for the exam, unless it was a very serious accident, infirmity or death of some close relative.

A student sitting at the back of the classroom asked with irony:

"Can we include fatigue from extreme sexual activity among the justifications?"

The classroom burst into laughter

The teacher looked at him and replied:

"Look, this cannot be an excuse. The test will be written, so you can easily come and write with the other hand. And there will be no problem if you want to do it standing up, if you can't sit down."

Appendix

I hope that thanks to my book you will be able to live more peacefully by taking back the power of the choices in your life, freeing yourself from all the commitments that do not interest you.

If you are wondering why in any of the chapters there are no 100 excuses as per the title, it is abundantly explained in Chapter 3

Notes on the author

May Betom Horrow

Writer, actor, director, musician, proofreader, editor, producer, screenwriter, editor, supervisor and asset, always with an excuse ready not to get the job done. Born listless in 1977 in Paris, after his studies, which he does not follow, he moved to Los Angeles in 2000 where he avoids doing anything. In the vast literary world of short stories, novels, cinema and production, he distinguished himself for that brilliant flair and for his clever excuses that prevented him from doing any kind of work. His apologies for him enjoyed international success, and already in 2005 he was awarded the prestigious "Apology of pure emotions" award. Award that he does not collect because it seems that the car had left him on foot.

Thanks to Gadama who believed in this book